SUPER
SURPRISING
TRIVIA
ABOUT
VIDEO
GAMES

by Mari Bolte

CAPSTONE PRESS
a capstone imprint

Spark is published by Capstone Press, an imprint of Capstone
1710 Roe Crest Drive, North Mankato, Minnesota 56003
capstonepub.com

Library of Congress Cataloging-in-Publication Data is available on the
Library of Congress website.
ISBN: 9781669064848 (hardcover)
ISBN: 9781669071815 (paperback)
ISBN: 9781669064893 (ebook PDF)

Summary: Think you know a lot about video games? Prepare to know even
more about video game history, famous games and gamers, and esports.
You'll be surprised by how much you'll discover in this totally terrific book
of video game trivia.

Editorial Credits
Editor: Erika L. Shores; Designer: Heidi Thompson; Media Researcher:
Jo Miller; Production Specialist: Tori Abraham

Image Credits
Alamy: ArcadeImages, 7, 12, 14, INTERFOTO, 10, pumkinpie, 13;
Associated Press: Jae C. Hong, 20; Dreamstime: Emily743, 8, PixelParticle,
15, Tashka2000, 21; Getty Images: GUILLAUME SOUVANT, 24, Mario
Tama, 9, Matt Winkelmeyer, 27, picture alliance, 23, Sean Gallup, 16; NASA:
JSC, 29; Newscom: Photoshot, 28, ZUMA Press/Christopher Drost, 25;
Science Source: VOLKER STEGER, 22; Shutterstock: Bobnevv, Cover (top
right), CaptNorth, 17, Dean Drobot, 4, ElenaNoeva, 19, Friends Stock, 5,
Gorodenkoff, Cover (bottom left), J. Helgason, Cover (bottom right), JOCA_
PH, 18, Mehaniq, 11, rafapress, 26, Voin_Sveta, Cover (top left), Shutterstock
Premier: The LIFE Picture Collection/Bernard Hoffman, 6

All internet sites appearing in back matter were available and accurate when
this book was sent to press.

TABLE OF CONTENTS

Words in **bold** are in the glossary.

DID YOU KNOW?

More than 3 billion people around the world play video games. Some do it for fun. Others compete in **esports** tournaments. There are quick, fun games you can play on your phone. There are also longer games with full stories. What you find out about video games may surprise you!

GOING OLD SCHOOL

Bertie the Brain was built in 1950. People could play a game of tic-tac-toe against Bertie. She was 13 feet tall. That's a little more than 28 iPhones high.

The first mobile phone game dates back to 1994. What was on the screen? *Tetris*!

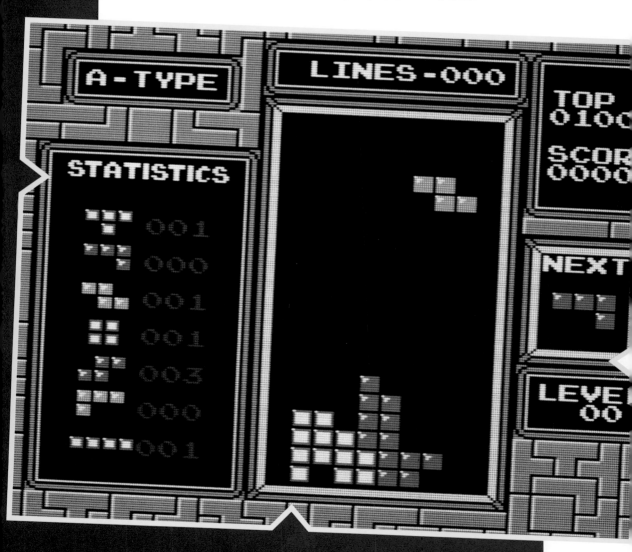

Computer Space was the first **arcade** machine. The creators went on to start the company Atari.

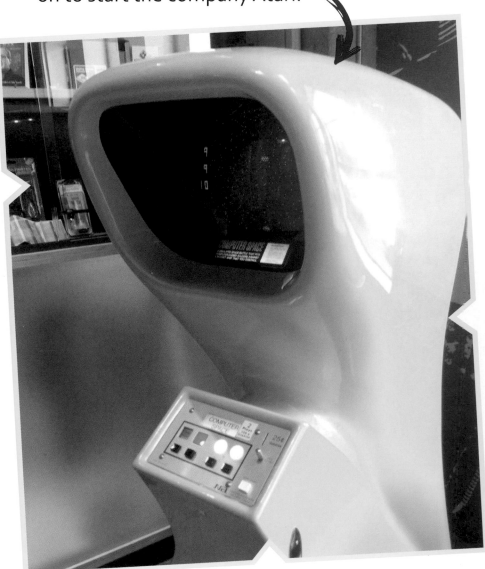

Dance Dance Revolution got arcade gamers moving. In 2011, Alexander Skudlarek broke a world record. He played DDR for 16 hours, 18 minutes, and 9 seconds.

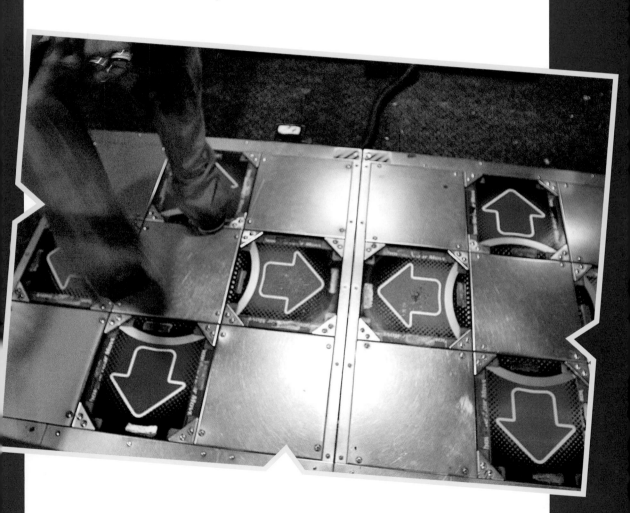

PLAYING AT HOME

The first video game **console** was the
Magnavox Odyssey. It came out in 1972.
All its games were ball-and-paddle games
similar to *Pong*.

It's Sonic versus Mario! Sega and Nintendo fought for the top spot in peoples' homes in the late 1980s and early 1990s.

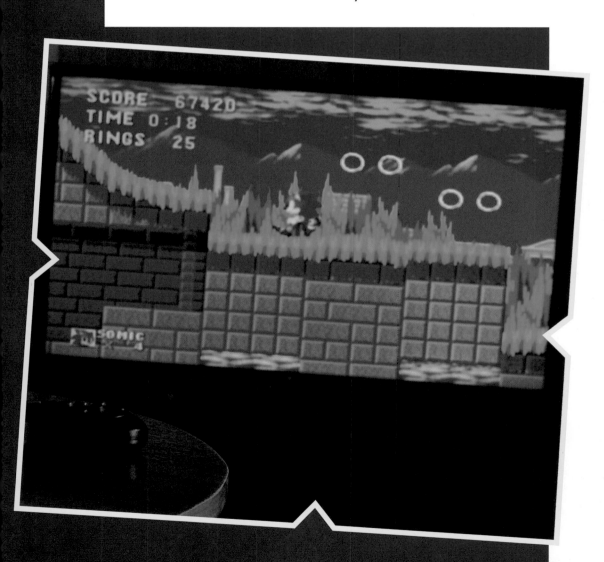

Sonic the Hedgehog 2 hit the shelves on Tuesday, November 24, 1992. It was the first time a game went on sale around the world on the same day. People called it Sonic 2sday.

Super Mario is the best-selling video game series ever. *Super Mario Bros.* has sold more than 40 million copies alone.

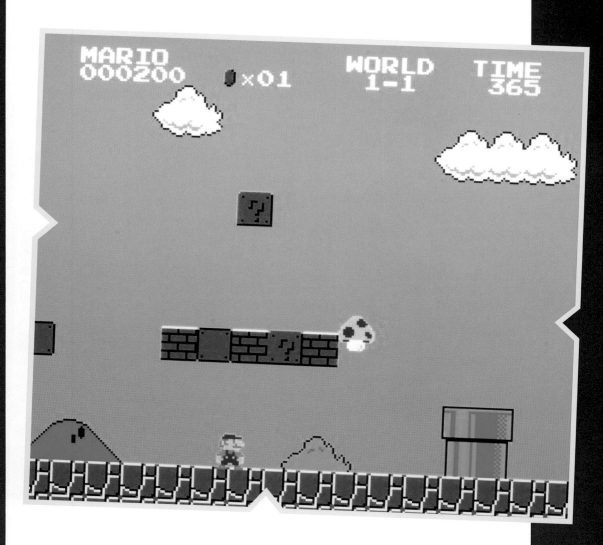

THE NEXT GENERATION

In 1999, *EverQuest* broke the internet—literally. So many people wanted to play the 3D game that the *EverQuest* **servers** crashed constantly.

In 2005, a **pandemic** struck *World of Warcraft*. It led real scientists to wonder if games like *WoW* could help understand actual **outbreaks**.

The first modern console war took place from 2005 to 2006. The Nintendo Wii, PlayStation 3, and Xbox 360 all had high definition graphics.

Microsoft Xbox 360

Final Fantasy XI was the first cross-platform game. People could play it on Xbox 360, PlayStation 2, and PC.

Minecraft was made in 2009. It took the creator less than a week to build.

Minecraft has sold more than 238 million copies. It is the second best-selling game of all time. *Tetris* is number one.

Amiibos are in. But they're not the first toys to work with games. In 2011, *Skylander: Spyro's Adventure* came out with **minifigures**. The figures gave players special powers or items.

Angry Birds was downloaded 500 million times in its first two years. It was played for 300 million minutes every day.

The first esports competition took place in 1972. Students at Stanford University competed in the Intergalactic *Spacewar!* Olympics.

Spacewar! was created on the DEC PDP-1 computer in 1962.

In 2019, the top-earning esports player was Johan "N0tail" Sundstein. He won $7.2 million playing *Dota 2*.

Esports competitions are not split into men's and women's divisions. There are no studies showing any differences in the way men and women play video games.

Sasha Hostyn

The top-earning female gamer is Sasha "Scarlett" Hostyn. Her game of choice is *StarCraft II*.

Twitch is a popular **streaming** service today. But the first streamer dates back to 1993. Twelve-year-old gamer Zot the Avenger played live on a public access channel.

One of the most-watched streamers is xQc. All combined, viewers spend more than 13 million hours each month watching xQc's Twitch channel.

In 2011, Kurt J. Mac set out on a journey to Minecraft's Far Lands. By April 2022, he had traveled 5,765,878 blocks. That was about 45 percent of the way.

Video game technology is being used to train astronauts going to the moon and Mars.

Glossary

arcade (ar-KAYD)—indoor areas containing coin-operated video games

console (KAHN-sohl)—a device used to play video games

esports (EE-sports)—video games played at a competitive level; esports is short for electronic sports

minifigure (MIN-ee-fig-yuhr)—a small plastic figure

outbreak (OWT-brayk)—when a number of people get sick at the same time from the same germ source

pandemic (pan-DEM-ik)—a disease that spreads over a wide area and affects many people

server (SUR-vur)—a large and powerful computer that connects other computers in a network

streaming (STREE-ming)—viewing over a computer network

Read More

Bolte, Marissa. *Super Mario*. Chicago: Norwood House Press, 2022.

Galanin, Denis. *The Amazing World of Video Game Development*. Reedley, CA: Familius LLC, 2022.

Koestler-Grack, Rachel A. *Curious About Minecraft*. Mankato, MN: Amicus, 2024.

Internet Sites

Facts Just for Kids: Video Game Facts for School
factsjustforkids.com/technology-facts/video-game-facts-for-kids/

Kiddle: Video Game Facts for Kids
kids.kiddle.co/Video_game

Index

About the Author

Mari Bolte is an author and editor of children's books on every imaginable subject. She lives in Minnesota, spending long winters with a Nintendo controller in her hand.